Welcome to Planet Reader!

Invite your child on a journey to a wonderful, imaginative place—
the limitless universe of reading! And there's no better traveling
companion than you, the parent. Every time you and your child read
together you send out an important message: Reading can be rewarding
and *fun*. This understanding is essential to helping your child build the
skills and confidence he or she needs as an emerging reader.

Here are some tips for sharing Planet Reader stories with your child:

Be open! Some children like to listen to or read the whole story and
then ask questions. Some children will stop on every page with a
question or a comment. Either way is fine; the most important thing
is that your child feels reading is a pleasurable experience.

Be understanding! Sometimes your child might need a direct answer.
If he or she points to a word and asks you to tell what it is, do so.
Other times, your child may want to sound out a word or stop to figure
out a sentence independently. Allow for both approaches.

Enjoy! This book was created especially for your child's age group.
Talk about the story. Take turns reading favorite parts. Look at how
the photographs support the story and enhance the reading experience.

And most of all, enjoy your child's journey into literacy. It's one of the
most important trips the two of you will ever take!

To Ryan and Dylan – E.M.

The author would like to thank
William A. Hazel, Inc., Chantilly, Virginia,
for their courtesy, enthusiasm,
and assistance in this project.

Copyright © 1999 by Elaine Moore.

Published by Troll Communications L.L.C.

Planet Reader is an imprint of Troll Communications L.L.C.

Printed in the United States of America.   ISBN 0-8167-6319-4

10 9 8 7 6 5 4 3 2 1

SEE YOU LATER, EXCAVATOR

Elaine Moore

Troll

Hey! What's happening?

Wow! Look at all that dirt!

track loader

Hold still, drill!

drill

9

Let's go, backhoe!

backhoe

CAT 10074

10074

CAT 963

NO RIDERS

Start your motor, track loader.

track loader

Move in closer,
sheepsfoot dozer.

sheepsfoot dozer

Make it smoother, earth mover.

earth mover

CATERPILLAR

30683

621

dump truck

Don't get stuck, dump truck.

roller

Roll it flat, just like that.

It's hard work, moving dirt.

bulldozer

But work is better when you do it together.

bulldozer

earth mover

Whew! All through.

earth mover

See you later, excavator.

excavator

dump truck

On to the next job.